T0040231

LAND OF SPIRITS

AN **UNOFFICIAL** COLORING BOOK

LAND OF SPIRITS

This book is not associated with or authorized or approved by
Hayao Miyazaki, his publishers, or Studio Ghibli.

Copyright © 2023 Ulysses Press and its licensors. All rights reserved. Any unauthorized duplication in whole or in part or dissemination of this edition by any means (including but not limited to photocopying, electronic devices, digital versions, and the internet) will be prosecuted to the fullest extent of the law.

Published by:
Ulysses Press
PO Box 3440
Berkeley, CA 94703
www.ulyssespress.com

ISBN: 978-1-64604-588-4

Printed in the United States by Kingery Printing Company
10 9 8 7 6 5 4 3 2 1

IMPORTANT NOTE TO READERS: This book is an independent and unauthorized fan publication. No endorsement, license, sponsorship, or affiliation with Hayao Miyazaki, his publishers, or Studio Ghibli, or other copyright or trademark holders is claimed or suggested. All references in this book to copyrighted or trademarked characters and other elements of Studio Ghibli are the property of their respective owners and used for informational purposes only. All trademarked products that appear in the book are the property of their respective owners and used for informational purposes only. The author and publisher encourage readers to watch, rent, purchase, and support Studio Ghibli, and to patronize the brands pictured in this book.

ビール
冷えてます。
ホッピー

ABOUT THE ILLUSTRATOR

Suhendra is a graphic artist specializing in nature, fantasy, and animal illustrations as well as original NFTs. He lives in Yogyakarta, Indonesia.

Discover More Great Coloring Books from Ulysses Press

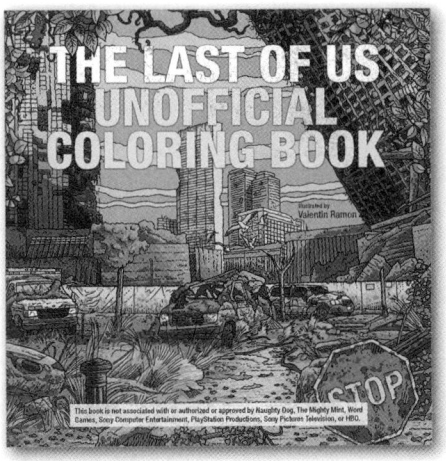

www.ulyssespress.com/coloring